Hadi Almenhali

4G Mobile Technology Features and Benefits for Business Solution

Hadi Almenhali

4G Mobile Technology Features and Benefits for Business Solution

LAP LAMBERT Academic Publishing

Impressum / Imprint

Bibliografische Information der Deutschen Nationalbibliothek: Die Deutsche Nationalbibliothek verzeichnet diese Publikation in der Deutschen Nationalbibliografie; detaillierte bibliografische Daten sind im Internet über http://dnb.d-nb.de abrufbar.
Alle in diesem Buch genannten Marken und Produktnamen unterliegen warenzeichen-, marken- oder patentrechtlichem Schutz bzw. sind Warenzeichen oder eingetragene Warenzeichen der jeweiligen Inhaber. Die Wiedergabe von Marken, Produktnamen, Gebrauchsnamen, Handelsnamen, Warenbezeichnungen u.s.w. in diesem Werk berechtigt auch ohne besondere Kennzeichnung nicht zu der Annahme, dass solche Namen im Sinne der Warenzeichen- und Markenschutzgesetzgebung als frei zu betrachten wären und daher von jedermann benutzt werden dürften.

Bibliographic information published by the Deutsche Nationalbibliothek: The Deutsche Nationalbibliothek lists this publication in the Deutsche Nationalbibliografie; detailed bibliographic data are available in the Internet at http://dnb.d-nb.de.
Any brand names and product names mentioned in this book are subject to trademark, brand or patent protection and are trademarks or registered trademarks of their respective holders. The use of brand names, product names, common names, trade names, product descriptions etc. even without a particular marking in this work is in no way to be construed to mean that such names may be regarded as unrestricted in respect of trademark and brand protection legislation and could thus be used by anyone.

Coverbild / Cover image: www.ingimage.com

Verlag / Publisher:
LAP LAMBERT Academic Publishing
ist ein Imprint der / is a trademark of
OmniScriptum GmbH & Co. KG
Heinrich-Böcking-Str. 6-8, 66121 Saarbrücken, Deutschland / Germany
Email: info@lap-publishing.com

Herstellung: siehe letzte Seite /
Printed at: see last page
ISBN: 978-3-659-78823-9

Zugl. / Approved by: Higher College of Technology , Abu Dhabi, UAE

4th Generation Mobile Technology Features and Benefits for Business Solutions

ABSTRACT

The rapid increase and the use of multimedia streams over the past decades have led to a change in the multimedia and mobile technology.

There has been a generational shift in the field of telecommunication and mobile systems that led to a major change and technology drift in many aspects.

The revolution of telecommunication and the utilization of IP telephony created a base of enhancement in the telecom field which enables the researchers in the field to quickly move from stage to other providing higher and reliable technology.

This paper describes the aspects which affect the streaming of video with regards to 4G technology. There are three aspects of streamlining video for faster transmission which will be discussed, these are; video compression, processor performance and 4G concepts.

The purpose of this report is to reveal the influence of 4G on the wide sector of business market in UAE. The question in this new domain is focused on the environment of UAE whether business and society are ready and willing to take and accept 4G as a replacement as soon as it is available. The author believes strongly that this technology and its features will benefit business and users and majority will welcome it in appositive way.

Glossary

Term	Stands For	Function
MPEG	Moving Pictures Experts Group).	A standard technology and format for compression of a sound and video sequence into a very small file (about one-twelfth the size of the original file) while preserving the original level of sound quality when it is played.
VCEG	Video Coding Experts Group	Responsible for standardization of the "H.26x" line of video coding standards
MVC	Multi-View Controller	MVC, or model view controller, is a technique used in software. Its fundamental purpose is to build a distinction between the way the software handles data, and the way the software interacts with the user
DSP	Digital Signal Processors	The goal of DSP is usually to measure, filter and/or compress continuous real-world analog signals. The first step is usually to convert the signal from an analog to a digital form, by *sampling* it using an analog to digital converter (ADC), which turns the analog signal into a stream of numbers
SD	Standard Definition	Video Definition or clarity signal that is used in digital TV. SD requires lower processor performance
HD	High Definition	Video Definition or clarity signal that is used in digital TV. SD requires higher processor performance.
FPGA	Field Programmable Gate Array	To reduce the computational load on a single processor. FPGA can be used in conjunction with DSP. The higher computational

		components can be done on the DSP whilst the FPGA can handle other processing needs.
CSC	Color Space Conversion	Color space conversion is required when transferring data between devices that use different color space models.
QoS	Quality of Service	To ensure quality of service
IP	Internet Protocol	Internet Protocol used for internet communication and addressing
WiMAX	Worldwide Interoperability for Microwave Access	Fixed wireless standard IEEE 802.16 that allows for long-range wireless communication at 70 Mbit/s over 50 kilometers. It can be used as a backbone Internet connection to rural areas.
UMTS	Universal Mobile Telecommunications System	The European term for third-generation mobile cellular systems or IMT-2000 based on the W-CDMA standard.
OFDM	Orthogonal Frequency Division Multiplexing	A method of digital modulation in which a signal is split into several narrowband channels at different frequencies in order to minimize interference among channels that are close in frequency.
SDR	Software-defined Radio	A radio communication system which uses software for the modulation and demodulation of radio signals.
TD-SCDMA	Time Division Synchronous Code Division Multiple Access	A 3G mobile telecommunication standard, being pursued in China by the Chinese Academy of Telecommunications Technology (CATT), Datang and Siemens AG, in an attempt to develop home-grown technology and not be "dependent on Western technology".
MIMO	multiple-input and multiple-output	is the use of multiple antennas at both the transmitter and receiver to improve communication performance

LTE	Long Term Evolution	LTE promises low costs, high throughput and low latency for a better user experience over older network technologies.
ITU	International Telecommunication Union	ITU is a United Nations agency that deals with telecommunications issues.
IEEE	Institute of Electrical and Electronics Engineers	IEEE is an international non-profit, professional organization for the advancement of technology related to electricity
CDMA	Code-Division Multiple Access	CDMA is considered "spread spectrum" technology which means that information contained in a particular signal are spread over greater bandwidth
E-UTRA	Evolved UMTS Terrestrial Radio Access	It is a key 3G technology to ensure the competitiveness of UMTS and provide a high-data-rate, low-latency and packet-optimized system.
UMTS	Universal Mobile Telecommunications System	is a third generation mobile cellular technology for networks based on the GSM standard
UTRA	UMTS Terrestrial Radio Access	combines circuit- and packet switching, to an all-IP system
3GPP	Third Generation Partnership Projects	The scope of 3GPP was to make a globally applicable third generation (3G) mobile phone system specification within the scope of the ITU's IMT-2000 project
VoLGA	Voice over LTE Generic Access	This Forum constantly committed to deliver the quality services of messaging service and also support for the voice by further expanding LTE technology over existing mobile networks
SCA	Software Communications Architecture	enables the parallel use of military, public safety and commercial radio networks

JTRS	Joint Tactical Radio System	JTRS is reconfigurable software-driven communications architecture (SCA) that aims to introduce a family of software-programmable radios, which will enhance communications capabilities and at a reduced cost of ownership.
AAA	Authentication, Authorization, Accounting	AAA servers in data networks are entities that provide Internet Protocol (IP) functionality to support the functions of authentication, authorization and accounting.
VPN	Virtual Private Networks	A method of encrypting a connection over the Internet. VPNs are used extensively in business to allow employees to access private networks at the office from remote locations. VPNs are especially useful for sending sensitive data.
FDMA	Frequency Division Multiple Access	FDMA is used exclusively for analog cellular systems, even though in theory FDMA can also be used with digital
	Frequency Division Multiple Access	A method of allowing multiple users to share the radio frequency spectrum by assigning each active user an individual frequency channel
IPSec	IP Security	IPSec provides security to IP flows through the use of authentication and encryption especially on WAN. It uses SSL VPN

Contents

ABSTRACT...2

Glossary..3

INTRODUCTION 8

Background Statement..8

Statement of the Problem...10

LITERATURE REVIEW..12

Background Theory..12

Video Compression 13

Processor Performance 15

4G Technology Concepts 17

4G Technology Functions 18

Long Term Evolution (LTE) Functions and Benefits 21

LTEs Provider's and Consumer Benefits 23

4G Integrated Processes..23

4G and Military Network:..25

4G benefits Summary:...28

RESEARCH METHODOLOGY 29

Discussion of Methodology 29

RESULT 30

DISSCUSSIONS & RECOMMENDATIONS...34

Discussions...34

Recommendations...37

Conclusion 38

REFERENCES 39

INTRODUCTION

Background Statement

These days, people rely upon mobile phones very much for voice calls/text messages and entertainment. Entertainment consists of media i.e. pictures, videos and audio. Video content on mobile phones have increasingly developed from short clips to short movies. While internet video streaming can take a long time, fourth generation (4G) technology can provide a solution by providing high data rates. Of all media types, transmission of video content is the most challenging as the amount of data for video content can be large. Streamlining the transmission of videos is important so that the end user can receive the video as quickly as possible, especially now that 3D television is emerging in today's technology.

As 4G technology is IPv6 based and provides higher data rates, streaming videos will become an attractive feature. This will revolutionise the way people watch videos on portable devices such as Mobile TV. Fast video transfer requires high speed data rates; hence 4G provides this feature however there are other factors which affect the streaming of videos which will be discussed later in the report, section titled Video Compression.

4G technology will be affecting the business of mobile phones services and will change the model of the classical mobile phone approach, thus the features and understanding of the old mobile phone services will be changing and the benefits of the technology will be enhanced. Features and benefits of 4G mobile technology will also be discussed later in the report, section titled features and benefits.

This study will explore the growing influence and reliance on mobile telephone technology, and how this concept is driving mobile telephone usage from voice to data and the challenge of streamlining video for faster transmission and delivery in 4G technology

The first Generation (1G) system was relatively new, albeit bulky, expensive, requires almost a small car battery, noisy and with limited communications output capability. A decade later, 2G was widely available to public with more base stations but the noise and battery consumption were negative issues due to the increase in use of mobile phones. The technology of 2G is analogue. In the 1990s, the 2.5G and 3G digital technology were introduced. They were far more enhanced version of mobile phones and their usage grew immensely in both industrial and developed countries.

Evolution from 1G to 4G:
Generations of mobile communication systems

	1st Generation (1G)	2nd Generation (2G)	3rd Generation (3G)	Beyond 3G / 4G
Timeframe	50s - mid 90s	90s - 2020?	2001 - ...?	in 10 to 15 years?
Technology	NMT, AMPS,...	GSM (worldwide), IS-95 (Americas, Asia), PDC (Japan),...	IMT 2000 , e.g. UMTS, CDMA2000	?
Standards	proprietary, domestic	A number of international standards	Few, open standards	One "umbrella" standard integrating heterogeneous technologies?
Bandwidth		Initially < 10kbps, evolves to 384 kbps	up to 2 Mbps	Yet more
A/D	Analogue radio, analogue /digital network	Digital	Digital	Digital
CS/PS	Circuit switched	Circuit switched	Circuit and packet switched	All-IP?
Cell radius	Up to 150 km	kilometers	Meters to kms	Meters to kms?
Mobility	Basic (national scope)	Advanced (continental scope)	Global (within same technology)	Global, intertechnology
Services	Speech	Speech, some data (MMS, SMS, WAP)	Speech, data, multimedia	All services, networking of networks, ubiquity,_

WS 04/05, TKN TU Berlin, Cornelia Kappler   Course UMTS-Networks, IV- Beyond UMTS

Table-1

The growing global demand helps how instrumental in elevating the mobile phone markets beyond the generation of voice and text further into multimedia. Multimedia

9

referred to as video and sound. The size of a file of a video is almost 1000 larger than the size of a sound file. Mobile phone hardware implementation is based on microprocessors. The technology of microprocessor has improved and still improving. Hence, 3.5G was introduced. The performance of 3.5 is impressive but still lacks quality when it comes to video usage, i.e. all current mobile phone are not practical to use multimedia communications (Glisic, 2003)

Statement of the Problem

What is the purpose of new generation mobile phones and why do we need to know more about it? Within the last 8 years, a group of companies agreed on non-published standard that would make multimedia usage on mobile phones practical with multimedia applications. For example, while the maximum bandwidth of 3.5G is 384 Kbps, (three hundred and eighty four Kbps) maximum 4G's bandwidth is 20 Mbps. This is quite adequate for large files with multimedia capacity (Glisic, 2009].

Currently 2, 2.5, 3 & 3.5Gs users pay per call/minute while 4G is basically an IP address based mobile phones. Thus there will be no limit to the usage as long as the user has got an IP address. There are more advantages with 4G over previous generations and potential for driving appreciable global market growth in coming decades.

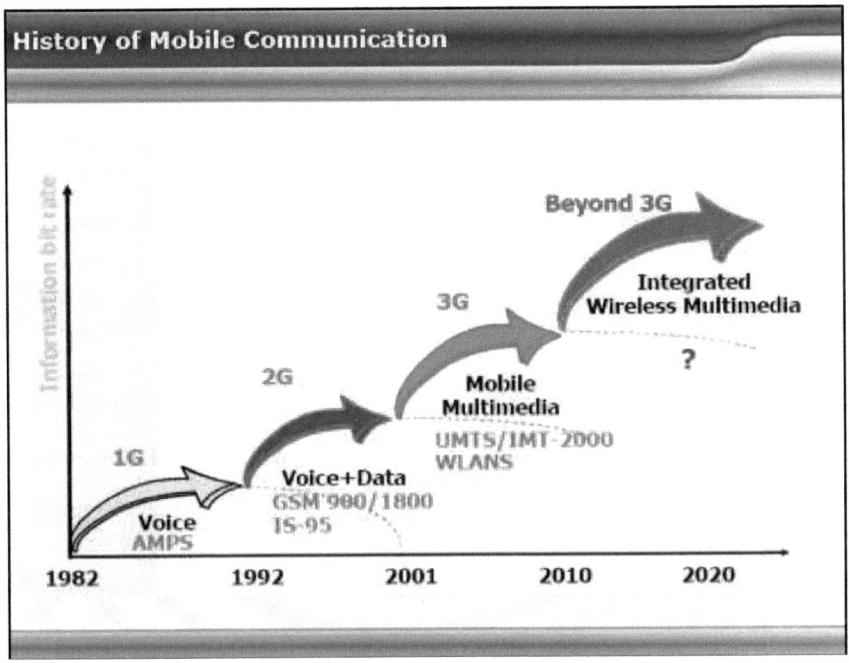

Illustration – 1 (History of Mobile Communication)

The business infrastructure of the current network companies will change. By becoming aware of, appreciating and understanding 4G technology, consumers will be better prepared to make more informed purchase decisions, resulting in higher consumer satisfaction and organizational effectiveness. The author posits that consumer 4G knowledge has obvious implications for the future marketplace competitiveness.

Question; who are the primary beneficiaries of 4G technology and what are the current trend makes the market place?

LITERATURE REVIEW

Even though this chapter could appear to be more technical but can be consider as a business because most of business benefits are technology driven and are direct result of technical output for any technology. Business benefit is driven by technology output and/or enhancement.

This section reviews technical and non-technical publications related to 4G technology as the aim is to highlight its distinguished and unique features and benefits as well as compare them with similar technology.

Background Theory

Originally the first generation (1G) cellular wireless technology was introduced in the 1980's. The 1G technology was analogue whereas the second generation (2G & 2.5G) was implemented as a digital system in the 1990's. In the 2000's the third generation (3G) was introduced [Camarillo 2008]. This is also a digital system, however compared with 2G technology, the data rates, bandwidths and other parameters have improved. It can be seen that each decade a new generation is introduced; therefore 2010's is the decade for the fourth generation (4G) technology. During the 1G era, the only service that could be offered was voice. Later, 2G & 3G offered voice and short messages. Sending media such as pictures was a huge advance in services to the end user however the speed was not favored as it took too long. As the technology advanced, the data rates have increased. 4G technology will be the era to provide high data rates for many applications including video streaming [Glisic, 2009].

This section reviews three topics, Video Compression, Processor Performance and 4G Concepts.

<u>Video Compression</u>

Video compression is needed because the raw video data uses a large amount of space (Effelsberg, 1999). Reducing the size of a video file can help with storage of the video as it will occupy less space on a hard-drive. It can also be helpful in the transfer of the data because less information needs to be transmitted. Moving Pictures Experts Group (MPEG) [Watkinson 2004] and the Video Coding Experts Group (VCEG) developed the algorithm H.264/AVC/MPEG-4 Part-10 (Luthra, 2003), a codec widely used in today's technology such as Blu-Ray discs.

The entire process of how a raw video signal is transferred so that it can be viewed on a display unit in a remote place (See figure 1). The raw (original) video signal is encoded using an algorithm such as H.264; this compressed signal can now be stored or transmitted to another location. Once the video signal has been received at the other end, the decoder decompresses the signal by using the inverse of the algorithm used to encode it. This will retrieve the original video signal which can then be displayed on the screen. (The signal might be affected by noise depending on the channel it has travelled through, however there are other components of the system which handle error correction).

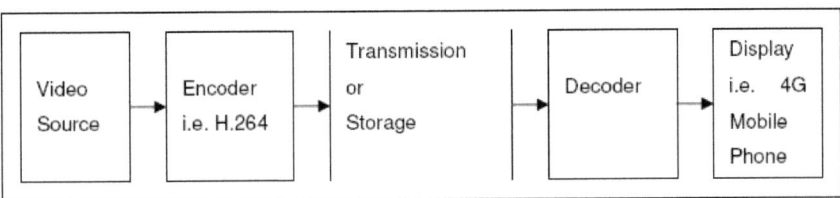

Figure 1 - Block Diagram of Encoder/Decoder

Figure 2 (Nuntius, 2009) shows the decoder which is the inverse of the H.264 algorithm. The inverse transformation is made here.

13

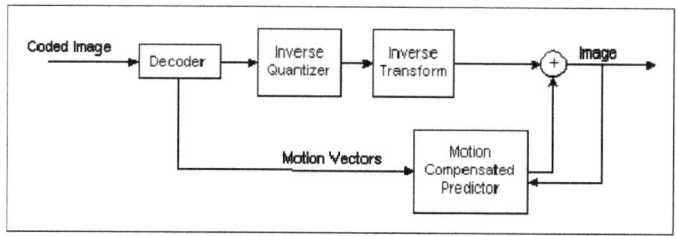

Figure 2 - H.264 & MPEG Decoder

There are many video compression formats available today, however high definition (HD) video content is widely desired in this era. High definition content uses the MPEG-4 (Part-10)/AVC/H.264 compression algorithm which allows for higher quality video whilst reducing the size of the data compared with the conventional DVD. H.264 is a licensed standard that supports the most efficient video compression technique available today (Axis, 2008). More recently, however, 3DTV has also emerged and has its own compression algorithm(s). While there may be various ways of implementing 3DTV, however, two methods are very popular; the stereo video method and the video plus depth method. Both methods require even more data than a normal 2D video signal. It is possible that the size of the video might be doubled as two video signals (left & right) will be needed, increasing the time it would take to stream a video to a 4G mobile handset. Currently, there are a few different proposals for compression of 3D video signals however these are not classified as standards yet. MPEG and VCEG have extended their MPEG-4 (Part-10) AVC/H.264 algorithm to MPEG-4 (Part-10) MVC/H.264. (MVC stands for multi-view coding). This algorithm converts multiple video signals into a single bitstream. This of course compresses the raw video signal which is a benefit for storage and transmission.

Although video compression does not relate directly to 4G technology, it will play a significant role as 4G technology can enable the viewing of large sized videos such as films, on a 4G mobile handset. Video compression will allow the size of the video to be reduced, hence transmitting less information for the same amount of data. It has been agreed on the fact that, the generations of the mobile phones have improved progressively and linearly with the improvement of the compression techniques. Research on the relationship between compression and quality and its fundamental application to 4G technology has been well established by [Weiss, 1993]; [Johnson 1999]; (Dipert, 1999) will apply to 4G as well.

Apart from compression algorithms, another aspect of streamlining video content for 4G mobile handsets is the processor which converts the received signal back to its original video signal. This will be discussed in the next sub-section.

Processor Performance

The type of processor discussed here is the processor that handles video signals. The performance of Digital Signal Processors (DSPs) used for compressing & decompressing video content is crucial for video transfer. The DSP needs to be computationally fast for decoding the bitstream for smooth playback. The increase in video resolution i.e. standard definition (SD) to high definition (HD) video has a higher performance requirement (Soohoo, 2005). Approximately 6 times more processing is needed for a HD video compared with the conventional SD video (Altera, 2007) which means that more data needs to be processed for each frame. This puts a heavy load on the processor which does the pre-processing/post-processing and decoding to convert the bitstream to a video. A heavy load on the DSP can increase the power consumption which is not ideal for mobile applications. Post-processing involves components which require high computation causing processors to use more power. To reduce the computational load on a single processor, a field programmable gate array (FPGA) can be used in conjunction with a DSP. The combinations of DSPs and FPGA coprocessors have become an attractive option for video processing (Soohoo, 2005). This method allows post-processing features to be processed separately on an appropriate processor, i.e. the higher computational components can be done on the DSP whilst the FPGA can handle other processing needs. Figure 3 shows the processing chains (Soohoo, 2005). The pre-and post-processing block diagrams are displayed to show how a FPGA co-processor will be used in this particular system. Scaling and colour space conversion (CSC) can be implemented on a FPGA. Whilst the DSP handles the more complex tasks, this reduces the latency, hence improving the time for video processing. Using the DSP & FPGA together is a good approach, however this increases the total power consumption, cost and size and therefore this method is not the ideal solution.

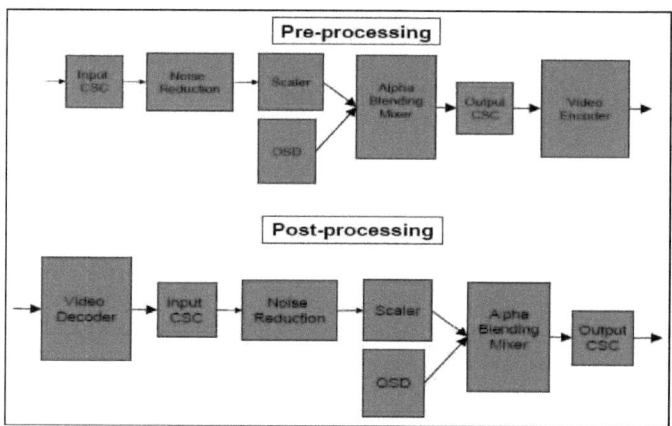

Figure 3 – Processing Chain

The RF (radio frequency) modules and RF amplifiers on the 4G mobile handset will require high performance as these handle the signals to and from the transmitter and receiver. If a video is being streamed from the internet on a 4G mobile phone, the incoming data must be received at a high rate so that the post-processing and decompression can take place in order to display the video content as fast as possible. In general, every component of the entire system which is involved in the data transfer must be of high performance. This will ensure that the streamlined video is transferred as quickly as possible. This means that the processor must have a high operating frequency for fast data transfer. The TigerSHARC processor by Analog Devices can reach data speeds of up to 384 kbps and also have multiple channels. Varying the use of the multiple channels can increase the data transfer rates (TigerSHARC, 2009).

Currently the TigerSHARC DSP is the most desirable for 4G applications and is widely regarded as the best suited processor for 4G technology as a whole. This processor includes special hardware operations so that it can work with different mobile networks and adapt to different telecommunication standards such as WCDMA. It is very flexible and allows compatibility for incorporating newer standards in the future (TigerSHARC 2009a). The TigerSHARC processor (TigerSHARC 2009b) will be able to provide the necessary performance required by 4G due to the high data handling rates. This will ensure seamless video streaming without the need of buffering compared to conventional methods.

4G Technology Concepts

To fully understand the benefits from 4G technology it is imperative to comprehend its operational functions, and consequent integrated role within other technologies.

The 4G concept as referred to in so many studies and literatures is based on the assumption that "the user has the freedom and flexibility to select any desired service with reasonable QoS and affordable price, anytime, anywhere." (Bojkovic, 2005)This technology is not one defined technology or standard, but a collection of technologies and protocols that are creating full packet-switched networks optimized for data and transparent integration, seamless mobility of heterogeneous access technologies, IP base core network and reconfigurable/auto configurable multi-mode, multiband terminals .

4G networks are projected to provide speeds of 100 Mbps on mobile or while moving and 1 Gbps on base stations. (Elias Aravantinos and M. Hosein Fallah, 2008)

4G expected outputs is high quality audio/video streaming over end to end internet protocol, therefore, if this produces what is expected, it will not matter what types of technologies used. WiMAX (Worldwide Interoperability for Microwave Access), LTE (Long term Evolution) or mobile structural design will become more transparent which will lead to enabling the operators to adopt several architectures.

Many Technologies appear in many different flavors and have many diverse tags attached to them, but that does not really indicate that they are moving in dissimilar tracks. The technologies that fall in the 4G categories are UMTS (Universal Mobile Telecommunications System), OFDM (Orthogonal Frequency Division Multiplexing), SDR (Software-defined Radio), TD-SCDMA (Time Division Synchronous Code Division Multiple Access), MIMO (multiple-input and multiple-output) and WiMAX to some extent. [Rysavy, 2009]

High data transmission is what is expected of 4G technology which will in turn generate new market trends for telecommunication businesses. With new 4G handset, built-in high resolution digital camera and High Definition capabilities will facilitate video blogs.

A successful implementation of 4G will most likely enable ubiquitous computing that will connect numerous data networks at one time with high data rates (100 Mbps for mobile users and 1Gbps for base stations) with desired QoS and faultless handoff. This will additionally enable many network operators to utilize different technologies, including cognitive radio networks to ensure desired bandwidth and secure connectivity. (Toshio Miki, Tomoyuki Ohya, Hitoshi Yoshino and Narumi Umeda, 2003)

4G Technology Functions

The need of fast, reliable and sufficient communication and quick data transfer is considered a priority of the present era as communication between businesses by sharing data becomes very important. Ever growing technology is the example of one such step towards the fastest possible transmission of data. 4G is the latest technology with high speed transferability of data with security measurements combined with wireless broadband for instant and fast download.

4G Technology is supposed to be based on two technologies namely.

Worldwide Interoperability of Microwave Access technology (WiMAX) and Long Term Evolution (LTE)

The International Telecommunication Union (ITU) promotes these technologies against the defragmentation and incompatibilities in 4G technology.
WiMAX, which stands for Worldwide Interoperability of Microwave Access, previously worked as a fixed wireless facility under the 802.16e band. Now the modified standard 802.16m has been developed with the properties of speed, wide spectrum, and increase bandwidth. (D. Rouffet, S. Kerboeuf, L. Cai, V. Capdevielle, 2005)

Since IEEE (the Institute of Electrical and Electronics Engineers) introduces WiMAX and releases it already therefore economic as no need to pay for its manufacturing price thus 4G has an advantage of having the WiMAX as a product supporting both WiMAX Network system (network infrastructure) and Mobile phone set.

Smart phones with Wireless Access are introduced in the market and are the model 4G mobiles. These smart phones are equipped with wireless internet accessibility and steady connection while traveling from one tower to another tower range.
Based on the IP wireless connectivity, it increases the optimization for the internet access. It manages the voice through packet-switching instead of circuit switching. Internet connectivity with specific IP not only increases the speed but also reliability of sending and receiving data, on key benefits for consumers. (M. Lazhar BELHOUCHET and M. Hakim EBDELLI, 2010)

Figure 4 – 4G LTE Terminal

The most common problem associated with connecting to WiMAX is the large amount of data transferred to the internet while spreading widely and fast across short bandwidth and narrow spectrum via a specific data carrier over the net. Arrival of 4G has diminished all the fears of lower bandwidth, narrow spectrum and amount of data send / receive. This WiMAX technology has a high data transfer rate with additional capacity for the subscribers and ready to carry a large amount of data. Previous generations were suffering because of low speed.

Parallel to WiMAX, LTE (Long Term Evolution) is introduced. LTE which is developed on radio wave technology is considered to be promising high data transfer speed and supposed to provide internet facility using both systems and also has the ability of transition from one mode to another. LTE not only increases the speed but also the amount of data allowed through the same bandwidth and results in lower cost and also has the compatibility of 3G technology therefore no new network infrastructure is needed.

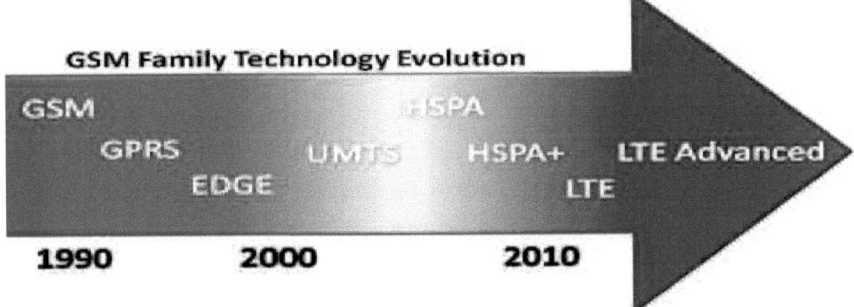

Figure 5 – LTE Evolution

As LTE is compatible with 3G technology it not only increases the speed but also eliminates the need for a new network as it can utilize the same network infrastructure. LTE is using MIMO (multiple input multiple output) and able to send and receive huge amounts of data and will never overload the base stations networks.

<u>Long Term Evolution (LTE) Functions and Benefits</u>

LTE is a new 4G technology that offers enhancements to existing mobile technologies and provides quality of service (QoS) as compared to other 3G and Wimax technology. LTE is widely called the competitor technology to WiMAX because of its wireless nature and mobile services. During the period of 2009 most of the mobile phones and other mobile broadband services operated on conventional GSM (Global System for Mobile communication) and CDMA. Now LTE offers lower cost for users of mobile wireless with high data speed and improved bandwidth for network service providers.

LTE Advanced technology offer network providers a reliable solution to migrate from 3G to 4G technology infrastructure. For mobile wireless users LTE facilitates the current applications to perform at better speed as well as for the new mobile applications to get more by using LTE.

LTE also referred to as Evolved UMTS Terrestrial Radio Access (E-UTRA), is currently being defined to replace the UMTS third-generation system. LTE-Advanced, in turn, refers to the most advanced version of LTE that was initiated about one year ago. LTE represents a radical new step forward for the wireless industry, targeting order-of-magnitude increases in bit rates with respect to its predecessors by means of wider bandwidths and improved spectral efficiency. Beyond the improvement in bit rates, LTE aims to provide a highly efficient, low-latency, packet-optimized radio access technology offering enhanced spectrum flexibility. The LTE design presents radical differences at every layer. Like many other communication technologies (e.g., digital video and audio broadcasting, DSL, wireless LANs), the physical layer uses OFDM waveforms in order to avoid the intersymbol interference that typically arises in high bandwidth systems. In terms of radio access, CDMA has given away to time and frequency multiple accesses. One differentiating aspect of the LTE standard is that from the onset, Multiple-Input and Multiple-Output (MIMO) is an integral component, and not an add on feature. At the network layer, a flatter architecture is being defined that represents the transition from the existing UTRA network, which combines circuit- and packet switching, to an all-IP system (al.}, 2009)

The major disadvantage of LTE is the cost of setup of new network infrastructure and in case of network upgrades; new equipments will be needed to be installed. Because LTE technology employs MIMO technology that raises the need to use additional antennas at network base stations for data transmission, users need to buy new cell phones to make use of new network infrastructure.

Third Generation Partnership Projects (3gpp) is the Industry group that aims to provide LTE standards. 3GPP group first introduced LTE to provide data transfer and afterwards mobile equipment manufacturers and mobile network providers joined this group in 2009 to build new shape of Voice over LTE by using VoLGA (Voice over LTE Generic Access) Forum. This Forum constantly committed to deliver the quality services of messaging service and also support for the voice by further expanding LTE technology over existing mobile networks. The basic agenda of 3GPP group is to create a transition friendly technology that can be easily deployed on the existing networks without any need of new network setups.

LTEs Provider's and Consumer Benefits

Another advantage of LTE technology is that it will lend a hand to 3G network service providers CDMA and GSM via current spectrum and increase their workability by speed up to 20 mbps as using the radio wave mechanism. It will not clash with the 3G services and will be able to use the same infrastructure for its functions.

It is under consideration that LTE's independent set up will enhance the proficiency of data transferring with additional features such as TV and multimedia applications. From a business prospective it will take new dimensions, you can think about having a mobile office. LTE technology will provide a platform for the different departments of a worldwide business at one point through mobile internet.

The feasibility of using any service any time will not only facilitate all the 3G features but also newest features, it will seem like a complete notebook considered as a mobile office. LTE technology will provide a type of switching method with the help of which you can move from one service to another using different function without any interruption. Gaming would be possible with 3D effects to augment the thrill and excitement. With the ease of using any service as per need, it will facilitate the use of different application at a time.

4G Integrated Processes

Reconfigurable Technology, IP Technology and Agent Technology in 4G are main and integrated element to enhance and ensure 4G services with best quality of service (QoS), high performance and low latency.

Each of these technologies provides and executes certain types of services to deliver the expectation of 4G. One of the most difficult problems is the receiving of IP packets while the process of handover finished in IP mobility, is how to ensure constant QoS level during the handover (Horizontal or Vertical) regardless whether the new access is in the same or other sub network. This has been identified as a handover latency which has great influences on the flow of multimedia application on the real time. The field "traffic class" and "flow label" in IPv6 header enable the routers to secure the special QoS for specific packet series with marked priority (Bojkovic, 2005). In order to utilize varieties of services and wireless network multimode user terminals are essential as they can adopt different wireless network to reconfigure themselves.

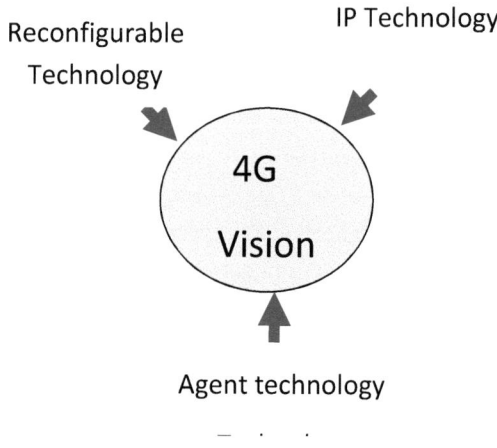

Figure 6 – 4G Vision

4G and Military Network:

Currently military fixed network are using commercial standards, hence evolving towards all-IP solutions and IP-supports. While military networks and commercial networks are converging COTS (commercial off the shelf), the ultimate goal of 4G mobile communication is to integrate all wireless network to a combined network with seamless mobility.

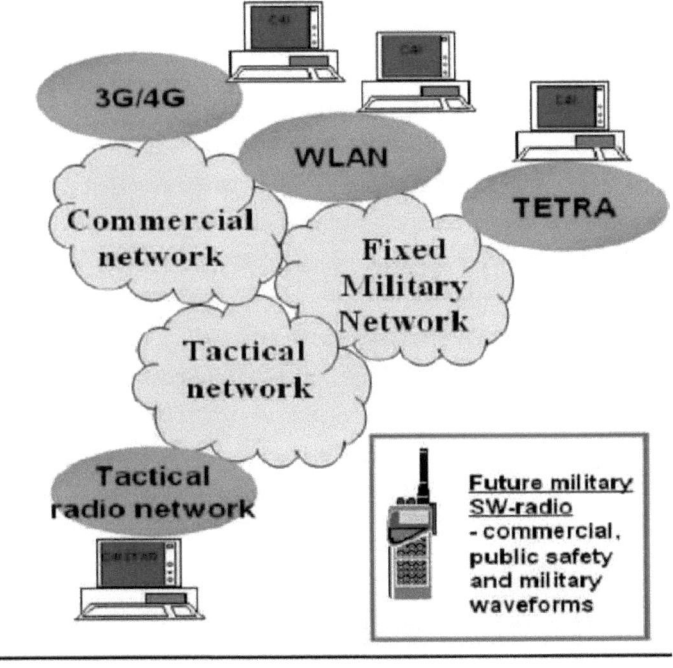

Figure 7 – 4G and Military Networks Integration

This seamless integration of future 4G heterogeneous networks is based on reconfigurable radios and IP mobility. 4G military software radio based on Software Communications Architecture (SCA) enables the parallel use of military, public safety and commercial radio networks, hence it can be implied that 4G military software radio is key enabler of 4G military communication. (Rantanen, 2003). Therefore, standardization co-operation between the military and commercial organizations might lead to common software radio architecture and benefits.

It is worth noting that the Joint Tactical Radio System (JTRS) program has been the definition of a software standard called Software Communications Architecture (SCA), intended to ensure portability of the waveforms across platforms from many vendors.

While SCA standardizes the software's operating environment, as well as the control and communication mechanisms for both the hardware and the external interfaces of the radio, in today's commercial network, security is becoming very tight and may meet the basic requirement of military communication network standard as it is always based on high quality end-to-end security. (Magazine, 2011). Many of the current and upcoming commercial techniques like Authentication, Authorization, Accounting (AAA), IPsec, Virtual Private Networks (VPN), XML electronic signature, could be adopted and adapted for military networks. The use of commercial radio access networks requires also specific implementation of Communication Security (COMSEC). (Rantanen, 2003). Closely associated with this topic is the vulnerability of the networks to counter-measures, jamming, denial of service attacks, intrusion etc. and the techniques to detect and protect against such attacks.

The co-operation of military and commercial organizations to develop open standards for fixed and mobile core network architectures will play an extremely important role in the future.

In principle, seamless mobility between military and commercial networks may be possible but needs co-operation at the standards level. Similarly, common standards for software radio architectures, such as waveform description languages, would have economical, operational and technical benefits. In reference with the enhancement in commercial network security an all other aspects, one can see the technical feasibility of commercial and military network merging especially when recalling the internet history and its military background.

The daily enhancement of all electronic technologies including IT, Networks and all other electronic related, the military usability of commercial networks becomes more understandable but I believe that policy and military sensitivity might be a barrier at least in near future.

In principle an Ad Hoc networking is the best solution for military radio communications. The main features of the ad hoc networks are communication without any fixed infrastructure, automatic set up of the network and adaptation to the networks architecture changes. In some cases the use of semi ad hoc networks may be more attractive. For example terminals set up a peer-to-peer network and multi-hop can be used for coverage extension to the overlay fixed network access point. However, in order to utilize the different military, and possibly in the future commercial, radio access networks multi-band multi-mode terminals are needed. Software reconfigurable radio technology is the most promising solution to build such transceivers. In the future, commercial mobile core networks will be responsible for mobility using Mobile IP for macro mobility between different networks. Future tactical networks could also be based on the same principle, and ideally mobility between commercial and military networks should be possible.

In light of the foregoing exploration of 4G technology and its fundamentals application and benefits, the methodology section of this research well enable us to gain further insight into the prevalent business benefits and solutions or lack thereof.

4G benefits Summary

4G benefits for business solution can be summarized in few sentences at this stage even though researchers might be able to produce more with enhanced research and familiarization.

The result of 4G expected throughputs (100 Mbps to 1Gbps) depends on user's usage of mobile or base stations. High throughput, easy accessibilities to user's data and premises provides the user's ability to work remotely as if they are in their geographical location, whereby enhancing the user's productivity by ensuring the ability to access required resources at all times and ensuring correspondence to their business needs. Easing communication among societies is a key benefit, as it will enables researchers, students, professors and all academic personal to communicate remotely. This will enable correspondents to gain comfortable access to each other's with high quality services and regardless of time zone barrier. All other parties can benefits from 4G in their respective ways.

Service providers will also gain lot of benefits as they will be able to provide more services with higher quality of service and in most likely standardized technology. This benefit can also be extended to manufactures as member of business supply chain network.

RESEARCH METHODOLOGY

A related and rational methodology has been adapted with this report called survey. The survey is a customised set of questions that are related to the topic of the report. This report has designed and developed a specific survey and has been conducted on a sector of industry and different groups of people to study the influence of 4G on the industry with current trends and specifically future prediction.

Discussion of Methodology

Overview

The aim of this project is to investigate the benefits and implementation trends of the 4G technology for business solution. To gain further insight into this question this research is necessary.

It is anticipated that the transition from the current technology (3G, 3.5G) to 4G will be smooth and then the current technology will subsequently become obsolete. 4G will provide large number of facilities, some of them has not been implemented yet. There will be some degree of difficulties to use 4G. This may lead to exclusion in business and society.

For the purpose of this research, both primary and secondary data sources were used. A survey about 4G technology future and benefits targeted two types of users (normal users and executive users). Also a secondary data was collected from various sources including but not limited to text books, technical publications, and technical magazines, tabulate newspapers, and professional opinion of industry leaders and practitioners.

Surveys questionnaires consist of 20 questions and open discussion were administered to cross section of 12 managers and 288 users in selected UAE organizations, including governmental and parastatals, with a total response rate of 31%. This is with a view to determining current trends of 4G technology awareness, applications, and subsequent organization benefits.

RESULT

The figure below illustrates the survey outcome.

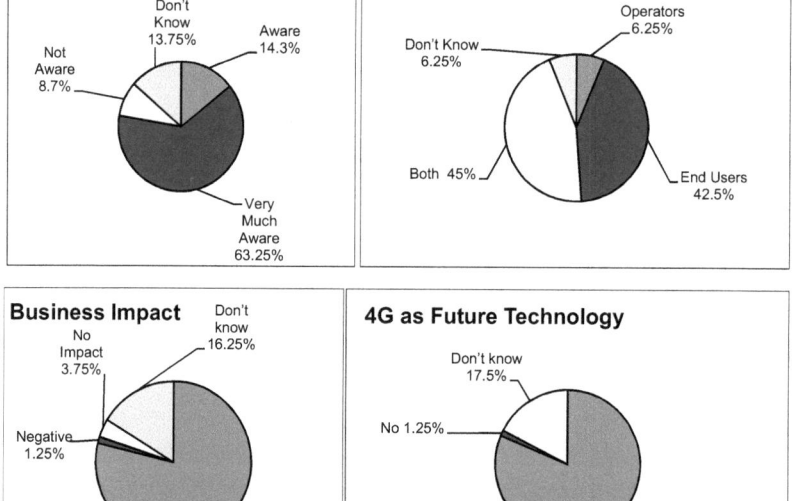

Figure- 8 4G Market Survey

4G technology seems to be promising for different types of users and been considered in market survey as a technology that could have a significant impact on business and normal users as shown on the survey curve. The above market survey figures shows how users expect the new technology to be and what impact it will have in users as well as business. Benefits are expected for both end users and operators in almost equal percentage and very positive business impact. This survey was administered among different group of professionals to sense the technology awareness and output expectation from different market users views. This survey has covered three types of user's categories, normal users, IT professionals and engineers, and medical field personal. It also covers business stakeholders or business executive.

Even though, it can be noted that engineers are more aware of the subject and have depth of technology knowledge but to certain extend, we can clearly sense the technology influence in the majority of normal non-technical users.

Normal users regardless of their educational level show superior knowledge or awareness of this technology even though it is not yet released. They have indicated in good level of precision the benefits expected from 4G and who will gain more benefit of 4G new features.

IT professional were much aware and demonstrate high level of knowledge about 4G technology. They highlighted their expectation of 4G technology feature, future and impact clearly and were very comfortable with new technology features. Their expectation of 4G technology market share and future was optimistic and nearly close to international researches expectation of 4G technology output.

Medical field personal also have shown good level of knowledge and have impressively demonstrate their knowledge and expectation widely regardless of participants percentage. They have clearly sense the benefits of this technology for medical field business.

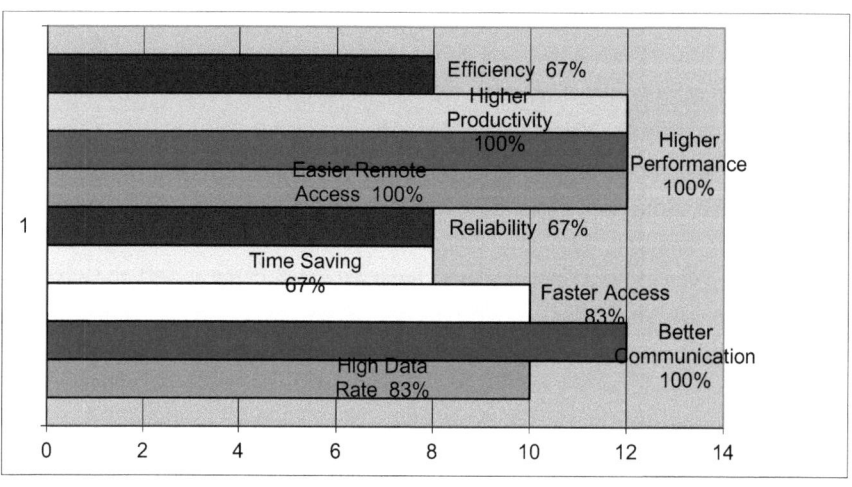

Figure-9 Executive Expectations

The Figures above shows the expected output of 4G from an executive prospective. More bandwidth will result in higher performance, easier and faster accessibility and higher productivity of organization as an output of smooth, quick and high throughput. An open ended question were hand-delivered to twelve executive including CEO (Chief Executive Officer), SVPs (Senior Vice President) and VP (Vice President) to explore their awareness of 4G technology and expectation of 4G output. Executive teams output to this research is important as executive always see business needs from a stratigic standpoint and have more understanding of business needs as well as future business requirements and challenges.

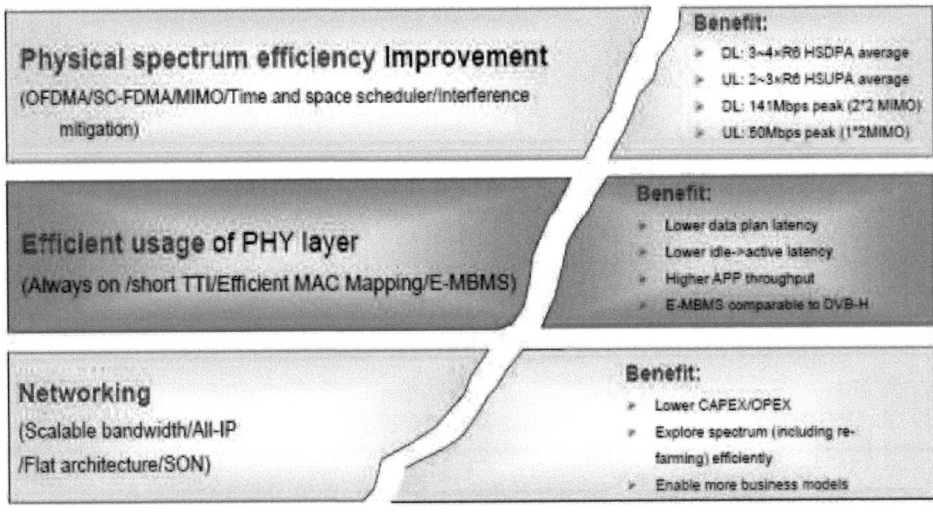

Figure-10

Figure-10 also provides more details of 4G benefits with much clearer definition of each benefit and how we gain that benefit.

It can be observed that improvement have taken place toward future mobile technology and that is explained in many ways. One umbrella standard integrated heterogeneous technology, all IP technology, and global intertechnology. All service networking (scalable network), efficiency usage of physical layer (low data plan latency, low idle active latency and higher app throughput) and physical spectrum efficiency (usage of OFDM-FDMA/MIMO time and space scheduler/interference mitigation). In view of figure-10 above, there is clear evidence of benefits attributable to 4G technology usage. Electronic data accessibility between individuals, groups or societies become simpler and faster. This will enhance all parties' capabilities to communicate, exchange experiences or knowledge and execute business needs smoothly whenever required even though not in one rounded table. 4G benefits will be described with more details in the discussion section.

DISSCUSSIONS & RECOMMENDATIONS

<u>Discussions</u>

To ensure clear understanding and provide clear direction of this discussion, the subject will be divided into two parts including survey output and secondary data sources output and expectation.

More specifically, the survey of UAE categories of users (executive and normal users) indicates the high quality, privilege and enhancement expectation of 4G technology for either business or normal users. At most, high performance, productivity, work enhancement and availability as well as easier, faster accessibility are expected output of 4G technology from a business prospective. From normal users prospective, better quality of service, fair and strong competition among operators, leads to cheaper price and customer focus are what 4G expected to deliver.

In glance of 4G technology survey for the UAE targeted costumers, users with respect to their professionalism background have shown great knowledge of 4G technology in regards of product awareness and benefits as well as business impact and that was a surprise of this survey. The targeted user's positive expectation output from 4G technology was a surprise as most of 4G features and benefits were expressed and expected to be delivered by 4G technology. High performance continues connectivity, market benefits of multi-provider and mutual benefits for both operators and users are what expected from 4G. The ability of this technology to sustain in the market as well as enriching the business with lot of facilities and positive impact is another surprise of the market survey. IT engineers are impressively showing great information of the technology and have illustrated high level of product awareness.

To streamline videos for 4G devices, two major aspects must be realised. These are the size of the file and processor performance.

The size of the file is of utmost importance as this can have a huge impact on the time it takes to transport/stream video data. It is therefore recognised that video compression is necessary. If a video was to be streamed from the internet using a 4G mobile handset, the hardware architecture on the handset must be capable of fast communication. This is so that the video can be streamed as quickly as possible. The second most important aspect is related to processor performance. The processor that handles the decompression of the encoded video signal must also be of high performance to enable it to execute the post-processing as quickly as possible. This will consequently reduce the latency between receiving the signal and displaying the video content on a screen. The processor itself has other factors which should be considered, some of these include power consumption and size as well as application that can run on it and how it integrates with other technology. (These are major topics which will not be included in this report but are stated to make the reader aware that other factors are also involved).

Mobile TV is soon going to become very popular as mobile phones are now becoming increasingly similar to personal computers. 4G technology is expected to provide a comprehensive IP solution where media (TV) and other services could provide the user any time anywhere (Wang, 2009). This means streaming video content from a shared server can also bring drawbacks due to bandwidth limitations.

Due to the increasing of business and individual requirement for connectivity and availability as well as Video streaming and with regards to the global shared interest, response time become a factor. Connectivity, availability and response time is driving the desire; therefore, 4G services are massively required to serve all the parties and satisfy individuals and business demand. With all functionality, services and quality of services of 4G, availability and rapid video streaming beside data downloads and uploads enables all parties whither business or individual, service provider or customers to be privileged.

This in depth analysis of the 4G system indicates significant benefits for all parties, including manufactures, service providers and costumers in different ways. Education, business, media, and individuals from a consumer prospective are benefiting from this technology as each of the mentioned parties could be served in suitable way that meets their requirement. An example of education is webinar, abroad classes and discussions on life video. Media could benefit on having the ability to broadcast instantly from the event site and in minimal equipment and with high quality signal. Business benefits of being able to communicate with other business counter parts at anytime whenever needed besides being privileged by having accessibility to their data as if they are in office. 4G provides a mobile office to all its business consumers and gives them the ability to get into their data with no latency or obstacles.

4G technology is going to be the future technology as it merges the voice, data and video services with high speed and quality of service (QoS). 4G with its security ability and availability also could privilege military users at least in ad hoc requirement if not fully. I believe the previous understanding of mobile or even phone technology in general is drifting from its old understanding to new arena and new business with totally new approach and services providing. Roaming service of mobile phone will disappear and also the one provider show in some regions will also have totally new challenges to deal with and have to look into the business from a sharing benefit for both parties (provider and consumer).

Recommendations

In accordance to business executive and normal user's survey output, 4G with its seamless connectivity, IPv6 technology, and all other integrated technologies there seems to be a promising future technology providing expected benefits in term of delivering all societies smooth communication. Connectivity, accessibility, high performance and availability are some of 4G features that attract the market and indicate the readiness of 4G market.

While compression techniques for HD video already seem to be the most efficient, however further research is needed to find more efficient methods of compression. The main task is to have a sufficient DSP which can decompress the encoded signal fro video applications. The TigerSHARC processor shown to be the most sufficient to-date with respect to flexible, and is capable of high speeds. The TigerSHARC ADSP – TS201S has a high performance of 500/600 MHz (TigerSHARC, 2009b). This processor seems the most efficient as it not only provides high performance, but it can be optimised for complex Digital Signal Processors (DSP) computations. As this processor is very flexible, it should be able to decompress video data regardless of what algorithm was used to compress it. This will be highly desired as the user will not be restricted to a small number of different formats as far as the processors concern. In consideration of military use, 4G with its seamless connectivity and integration with all other communication technology, the benefit and utilization of 4G for military usage is applicable in many aspects. 4G for business needs seems to be the future technology with all capabilities that will enable the users to connect anytime anywhere to the internet based on IP technology and communicate with any business community; therefore, 4G technology with its integrated elements sound to be the recommended technology for individual and business benefits. 4G systems give mobile users a virtual presence, always on connections to keep people on event (M. Lazhar BELHOUCHET and M. Hakim EBDELLI, 2010).

Conclusion

4G technology is a new approach of telecom and computing technology that will remain in service for long after its mature implementation. High audio/video throughput, QoS full packet-switched networks optimized for data and transparent integration, seamless mobility of heterogeneous networks meets markets need and will meet user's expectation of 4G in term of quality of services, performance and cost. Integration of multi vendor hardware and software, multi user (Commercial and Military) of 4G technology is another approach that will enable 4G to attract more customers and take over market that have been restricted or identified for certain players. With the concept of "the user has the freedom and flexibility to select any desired service with reasonable QoS and affordable price, anytime, anywhere." (Bojkovic, 2005) 4G will be the future technology.

While this research has uncovered specific areas of solutions attributable to 4G technology usage is no doubt the need for future research with respect to specific industries applications and/or new services additions for future users, and inherent challenges associated with user specialization.

It is also noteworthy to mention that while this research formally supports previous literature with respect to general benefits cluster (see figure10).

It has inbuilt limitation of time and industry-specific constraints. Perhaps longitudinal study would be more appropriate in the future.

REFERENCES

Altera Corporation (2007). Video and Image Processing Design Using FPGAs", White Paper,

Axis Communication (2008). H.264 Video Compression Standard – New possibilities within video surveillance. White Paper,

Dipert, B., (1999). *Digital Audio Breaks The Sound Barrier*, EDN, 20 July.

Effelsberg, W. & Steinmetz, R. (1999) "Video Compression Techniques: From JPEG to Wavelets" ISBN: 3920993136, Morgan Kaufmann, 9 Mar.

Frattasi, S.,et al. (2006). *Defining 4G technology form the user's perspective*. IEEE Network. January/February p. 35 (7).

Johnson, R., (1999). *JPEG2000 Wavelet Compression Spec Approved*, EE TIMES, 29 December.Koenen, R., (1999) *MPEG-4: Multimedia For Our Time*, IEEE SPECTRUM, pp. 26-33, February.

Luthra, A., Sullivan, G.J., Wiegand, T.,(2003). *Introduction to the special issue on the H.264/AVC video coding standard*, Volume: 13 Issue: 7, pp. 557 – 559,

Nuntius Communications (2009). H.264 – A New Technology for Video Compression. *<http://www.nuntius.com/technology3.html>* Accessed on: 26/03/10

Paragon, 2011 http://www.marketwatch.com/story/alcatel-lucent-and-powerwave-benefit-from-4g-shift-2011-10-25

Prehofer, C.& Wei, Q. (n.d.). Active networks for 4G mobile communication: Motivation, architecture and application scenarios. DoCoMo Communications Laboratories Europe.

Soohoo, A.(2005). "FPGA Co-Processing Architectures for Video Compression", Altera Corporation.

TigerSHARC (2009). "Why Choose TigerSharc Processors for wireless?", Analog Devices. <http://www.analog.com/en/embedded-processing-dsp/TigerSHARC/processors/why_TigerSHARC/fca.html> Accessed on: 26/03/10

TigerSHARC (2009a). TigerSHARC ADSP-TS201S, Analog Devices, Datasheet <http://www.analog.com/static/imported-files/data_sheets/ADSP_TS201S.pdf> Accessed on: 26/03/10

TigerSHARC (2009b) ADSP-TS201S, Analog Devices, Datasheet <http://www.analog.com/static/imported-files/data_sheets/ADSP_TS201S.pdf> Accessed on: 26/03/10

Wang H., Kondi L., Luthra A. & Ci, S.(2009). 4G Wireless Video Communications, John Wiley & Sons Ltd,: San Francisco.

Watkinson, J. (2004). The MPEG Handbook: MPEG-1, MPEG-2, MPEG-4, ISBN: 024080578X, Elsvier, 7

Weiss, J. & Schremp, D.,(1993). *Putting Data On A Diet*, IEEE SPECTRUM, August .

4G Evolution, 169 (May 30, 2008).

al.}, B. C. (2009). EURASIP Journal on Wireless Communications and Networking. 3GPP LTE and LTE Advanced , 167.

Bojkovic, Z. (2005). Fourth Generation Mobie system 4G.

D. Rouffet, S. Kerboeuf, L. Cai, V. Capdevielle. (2005). 4G Mobile. ALCATEL TELECOMMUNICATIONS REVIEW.

Glisic, S. G. (2003). Advanced Wireless Networks: 4G Technologies.
M. Lazhar BELHOUCHET and M. Hakim EBDELLI. (2010). ITU/BDT Arab Regional Workshop on "4G Wireless Systems".

Rysavy, P. (2009). 3GPP Broadband Evolution to IMT-Advanced (4G). Peter Rysavy, Rysavy Research.

Toshio Miki, Tomoyuki Ohya, Hitoshi Yoshino and Narumi Umeda. (2003). The Overview of the 4th Generation Mobile. NTT DoCoMo Inc., Wireless Labs.

Ari Hottinen, O. T. (2003). Multi-antenna transceiver techniques for 3G and beyond. In O. T. Ari Hottinen, Multi-antenna transceiver techniques for 3G and beyond (p. 323). John Willy & son td.

Consulta, R. R. (2007). 4G Mobile Networks - Technology Beyond 2.5G and 3G. Retrieved May 20, 2011, from 4G Mobile Networks - Technology Beyond 2.5G and 3G: http://snu-kr.academia.edu/RoyConsulta/Papers/81965/4G_Mobile_Networks_-_Technology_Beyond_2.5G_and_3G

Five Ways to Benefit from 4G Wireless Internet. (2009, Oct 18). Retrieved May 10, 2011, from http://www.articlesbase.com/internet-articles/five-ways-to-benefit-from-4g-wireless-internet-1351714.html#axzz1PXUrM22H

4G Broadband. (n.d.). Retrieved May 15, 2011, from 4G Broadband: http://www.broadband-expert.co.uk/4g-mobile-broadband/

Consulta, R. R. (2007). 4G Mobile Networks - Technology Beyond 2.5G and 3G. Retrieved May 20, 2011, from 4G Mobile Networks - Technology Beyond 2.5G and 3G: http://snu-kr.academia.edu/RoyConsulta/Papers/81965/4G_Mobile_Networks_-_Technology_Beyond_2.5G_and_3G

Aghvami, P. H. (2004). UMTS and Beyond. London: Kings College, London.

Rantanen, H. (2003). FUTURE MILITARY SYSTEMS

Magazine, N.D (2011). Army Continues Hunt for the Latest Wireless Technologies. http://www.nationaldefensemagazine.org/blog/Lists/Posts/Post.aspx?ID=499